21 QUESTIONS ABOUT OPENING A BREWERY IN THE UNITED STATES
A FEDERAL PRIMER

BY ANDA LINCOLN AND BRAD LINCOLN

PUBLISHED BY DARK TRAIN LLC.

DARKTRAIN LLC.
14525 SW MILLIKAN WAY #32450
BEAVERTON OREGON 97005-2343
WWW.LEGALBREWING.COM

VERSION USB1.4

ISBN-13: 978-0-9825841-0-1

PUBLISHER: DARK TRAIN LLC.
AUTHORS: ANDA LINCOLN AND BRAD LINCOLN
COVER PHOTO: ZAK ROTELLO

About 21 Questions About Opening a Brewery in the United States

We are a husband and wife team. In early 2008, we left our gigs as a CPA and an attorney to pursue our beer and entrepreneurial passions. We have always wanted to experience the gratification of creating a unique product and sharing it with others.

The idea for a series of Brewer's Primers to alcohol and beverage laws was sparked from our journey to open a small package brewery. We are currently working with a friend to open a package brewery in Fort Collins, CO. Before coming to Fort Collins, we put a lot of energy into determining the feasibility of breweries in Arizona, Vermont, and south Florida.

Unfortunately, after many hours of research, our business ideas for a small package brewery were often snuffed out by the minefield of federal and state laws and regulations. Then we thought: "Wouldn't it be great if there was a guide to the laws of each state?"

Such a guide would give brewers interested in opening or expanding breweries a quick glance at the issues they might face, and allow them to be more productive with business plans. So, we began to create our own series of primers to the alcohol and beverage laws affecting breweries in the Unites States.

Our Primers are focused on providing brewers with a basic understanding of what issues might arise in opening or expanding a brewery. They also help a brewer identify what questions to ask about the alcohol and beverage laws, and where to find the answers; thus, freeing the brewer to focus on generating innovative business ideas.

This Primer is the third Primer in our series. Instead of being focused on individual states, like our other products, this Primer is focused on the federal laws. It also gives a brewer an overview of things to watch out for at the state level when starting a brewery.

If you are a startup brewery, or an established brewery looking to expand, we are sure you will find our series helpful. We would appreciate any input you have on this product or any of our other products.

Thank you!

Anda & Brad Lincoln
support@darktrainink.com

Table of Contents:

What is alcohol control all about? Or, the perceived evils that lead to a legal maze.

The United States has an interesting history with alcohol control, leading to the adoption of the Eighteenth Amendment prohibiting manufacture, sale, and transportation of alcoholic beverages (it did not prohibit consumption outright). Prohibition was a means to control the perceived evils of alcohol, namely over consumption and crime. Prohibition as a means to control alcohol consumption famously failed. It only led to the rise of organized crime, bootlegging, and rum running; alcohol consumption even rose during the Prohibition years. The Twenty-First Amendment repealed the unpopular law thirteen years later.

The repeal of Prohibition returned power to the states to deal with the "evils" of alcohol. The goals of most states in enacting alcohol control legislation were to control consumption, eliminate crime, and raise state revenues. Some states focused more on certain goals of alcohol control than others. The resulting patchwork of archaic laws, both state and federal, attempt to meet alcohol control goals through state and federal licensing processes, mandated three-tier distribution systems, extensive background checks on license applicants, and excise taxes.

Prior to Prohibition, most manufactures and retailers were often vertically integrated; retailers selling alcohol to consumers were often owned by their upstream suppliers. The vertical integration model created lower prices for a retailer, and guaranteed a return to a manufacturer wanting to capture a certain market. This is still the distribution system widely used in Germany, Ireland, and other nations. Because this method is often more profitable, it created alleged excessive promotion of alcohol which led to alleged over indulgence.

The states and federal government, in order to deal with the perceived evils, opted to prohibit tied houses in the United States (manufacturers and whole-salers are generally prohibited from owning any interest in, or from providing anything of value to, a retailer). The states also created a three-tier distribution system whereby manufacturers are generally prohibited from selling to retailers and consumers, and may only sell to wholesalers.

The three-tier system is also intended to control crime in the industry. Criminal background checks at the state and federal level are used to keep persons with criminal convictions, or with financially unstable businesses, from opening or operating an alcohol based business. Many states prohibit anyone with a felony conviction, or with convictions for prostitution, violations of alcohol or other "moral" laws from obtaining licenses to run an alcohol based business.

Excise taxes, again both at the state level and the federal level, are also used to control the perceived evils of drinking and corruption. Excise taxes control the price of alcohol so that it does not become too cheap and easily accessible. These taxes also provide the state and federal government with a steady stream of revenue.

The patchwork of laws regulating the alcohol industry extend to advertising and label requirements and prohibitions. The alcohol industry cannot operate businesses the way other industries can. Even how an alcohol business can be purchased by a new owner is often controlled by the alcohol and beverage laws.

At a state level, there are "control states" and "license states." Eighteen states (the control states) have opted to control the sale of all or some alcoholic beverages (Alabama, Idaho, Iowa, Maine, Michigan, Mississippi, Montana, New Hampshire, North Carolina, Ohio, Oregon, Pennsylvania, Utah, Vermont, Virginia, Washington, West Virginia, and Wyoming). Some control states, such as Alabama, control all wholesale and retail sales of moderate and high alcohol content beverages (fortified wine and beer, and spirits). Others are hybrids; such as Oregon, which allows the sale of beer and wine by private enterprise. In control states, restaurants serving spirituous liquors must also purchase alcohol from the alcoholic beverage control board. The license states, on the other hand, have created complex licensing systems to allow private enterprises to sell alcohol to consumers. The licensing systems mandate three-tier distribution systems similar to the ones imposed in the control states, often with varying exceptions.

This publication is focused on some (but definitely not all) of the laws governing breweries and brewpubs in the United States. This publication is not (nor is it intended to be) an inclusive guide to the alcoholic beverage laws of the United States, or any state, the District of Columbia, or United States territories. It is provided for informational purposes only, and as an introductory guide to some of the general issues a brewer might face in starting and operating a brewery or brewpub in the United States. The state law examples provided throughout this publication are provided as illustrations of how divergently the states deal with the same alcohol control issues. The state law examples are not, nor are they intended to be, guides to how the states administer alcohol control laws.

When working with any laws, but especially alcohol and beverage laws, it is important to remember that even if an action is not explicitly forbidden by law or regulation (either federal, state, or local), the action may still not be allowed by the governing authorities. When in doubt, or moving into uncharted waters, it is best for a brewery to work with a competent licensed attorney and to contact the TTB and the alcohol board for the state in which it is conducting business.

Question 2

What are the laws that govern brewers and breweries? Or, where the headaches start.

The alcohol industry is one of the most regulated industries in the United States. There are federal laws, state laws, and local county and municipal laws that regulate the manufacture, sale, shipment, delivery, use, and even possession of alcoholic beverages. The various laws supplement each other. So, in any given city the federal laws, the state laws, the county laws, and the city laws will all apply. On a federal level, all brewers wishing to sell their beer need to be aware of at least the following groups of laws:[1]

- The Internal Revenue Code (the "IRC,") contained in the United States Code ("USC"), Title 26, Chapter 51;

- The Federal Alcohol Administration Act (the "FAA Act,") contained in Title 27 of the USC, Chapter 8;

---

[1]   Links to the federal laws can all be found at
         http://www.ttb.gov/beer/beer-regs.shtml

- The Federal Code of Regulations ("CFRs"), Chapter 27, Parts:

  - 6 (Tied House),
  - 7 (Labeling and Advertising of Malt Beverages),
  - 8 (Exclusive Outlets),
  - 10 (Commercial Bribery),
  - 11 (Consignment Sales),
  - 13 (Labeling Proceedings),
  - 16 (Alcoholic Beverage Health Warning Statement), and
  - 25 (Beer).

The CFRs set out the federal regulations dealing with all aspects of beer production and sale. There are specific rules for what a brewery can be used for, as well as beer formulas, label, and advertising regulations. Certain trade practices are also prohibited on a federal level, such as consignment sales, exclusive outlets, and tied houses.

Each state, the District of Columbia, and each United States territory has its own set of laws governing and regulating alcoholic beverages. The state laws are applicable not only to breweries located in those states, but also to breweries selling their out of state manufactured beer in that state. As a third, and sometimes fourth, layer of confusion, there are often additional county and municipal laws and regulations that apply to alcoholic beverages (such as sales taxes, time of day sales laws, and location regulations, among others).

Unfortunately, there is no uniform set of laws that apply throughout any two states (except for the federal laws that apply in all the states). The specific state and local laws are important to know before choosing a state in which to open a brewery. It is also important to consider different state laws when outlining a business plan that includes distribution of beer to other states.

The laws described in this publication are not the only laws a brewer needs to be familiar with in opening or operating a brewery. A brewer also needs to be familiar with other related federal laws and regulations on alcohol, as well as related state and local laws and regulations. The local laws (set forth by the states, counties, and cities) regulate everything from who is eligible to brew beer, to the time of day alcohol may be sold, and the building codes for constructing a brewery. The state, local, and federal laws are all equally important and need to be followed to be a successful law abiding brewery.

There are also additional federal, state, and local business laws, employment laws, advertising laws, insurance laws and regulations, water rights laws, contract and commercial laws, zoning laws, environmental laws, and tax laws, among others, that a brewer must be familiar with when starting and operating an alcohol based business in any state. All of these laws are beyond the scope of this publication. It is important for every brewer to obtain advice from a competent licensed attorney in his or her state before opening any kind of alcoholic beverage based business.

Question 3

Who is in charge? Or, where it would be nice to have a friend.

On a federal level, the Alcohol and Tobacco Tax and Trade Bureau (the "TTB"), is charged with administering the laws and regulations governing alcohol, tobacco, firearms, and ammunition, and to collect excise taxes on those products. There are divisions within the TTB that are responsible for the regulation and collection of excise taxes, for approving and regulating alcoholic beverage businesses, as well as for label and formula approval and regulation. There are regional offices responsible for the regulation of alcohol based businesses for groups of several states. Generally, a brewer will be dealing with the regional office responsible for his or her state.

The TTB's general contact information is:

E-mail: ttbquestions@ttb.treas.gov
Telephone: 202-453-2000
U.S. Mail: Alcohol and Tobacco Tax and Trade Bureau
              Public Information Officer
              1310 G Street, NW, Suite 300
              Washington, D.C. 20220

On a state level, each state has an alcoholic beverage control board or division. The state alcohol control divisions regulate the production, sale, shipment, use, and possession of alcoholic beverages. They provide licenses and collect excise taxes from alcohol based business.

A list of the alcohol control divisions by state and their contact information can be found on the TTB's web site at: http://www.ttb.gov/wine/control_board.shtml. Please note that the contact information on the TTB's web site is subject to change and may not always be the most up-to-date contact information for each state.

What is beer? Or, why beer in one state is not necessarily beer in another state.

The first step in determining how the alcohol laws apply to a brewery is to figure out what beer is. The definition of beer is important to understand because it determines which laws and regulations apply. In some cases, the definition will also determine how a brewery's product can be sold.

Beer is an alcoholic beverage containing water, malted barley, hops and yeast. Right? Of course, legislators have found many different ways to define beer. Each state, territory, and the federal government has a definition of beer.

Alcoholic Beverage

First, beer is an alcoholic beverage. An alcoholic beverage, as far as the federal government is concerned, "includes any beverage in liquid form which contains not less than one-half of one percent of alcohol by volume and is intended for human consumption." *See* §27 USC 214(1). Most states have a similar definition of alcoholic beverages.

Beer

Beer, or a malt beverage, under the federal laws is "a beverage made by the alcoholic fermentation of an infusion or decoction, or combination of both, in potable brewing water, [of] malted barley with hops, or their parts, or their products, and with or without other malted cereals, and with or without the addition of unmalted or prepared cereals, other carbohydrates or products prepared therefrom, and with or without the addition of carbon dioxide, and with or without other wholesome products suitable for human food consumption." *See* §27 USC 211(a)(7). In other words, beer is any "beer, ale, porter, stout, and other similar fermented beverages (including sake and similar products) of any name or description containing one-half of one percent or more of alcohol by volume, brewed or produced from malt, wholly or in part, or from any substitute for malt." *See* §27 CFR 25.11.

According to the federal regulations, beer must contain malt or malt substitutes (rice, grain of any kind, bran, glucose, sugar, and molasses). But, may also include fermentable and non-fermentable adjuncts (honey, fruit, fruit juice, fruit concentrate, herbs, spices, and other food materials). *See* §27 CFR 25.15(a). Flavors and non-beverage ingredients containing alcohol, can also be used to make beer, so long as these additives do not contribute more than 49% of the overall alcohol content of the finished beer. For example, a finished beer that contains 5% ABV may only derive 2.45% ABV from the alcohol containing flavors. *See* §27 CFR 25.15(b).

Cider and Mead

Cider and mead, since they are not made with malt, both fall under the federal wine definition. At a federal level, wine includes "sparkling and carbonated wine, wine made from condensed grape must, wine made from other agricultural products than the juice of sound, ripe grapes, imitation wine, compounds sold as wine, vermouth, cider, perry, and sake." *See* §27 CFR 1.10. Mead, made from honey, an agricultural product, is an "agricultural wine," or wine "made from agricultural products other than the juice of fruit." *See* §26 USC 5387.

Beer and the States

The state definitions of beer vary from state to state, of course. We have included below some examples of different variations on the state definitions. The definitions below are provided as examples only, and may not be used as guides to the state definitions of beer, cider, or mead. As previously mentioned, each state has its own definition of beer, and a brewery needs to be familiar with the definition in its home state as well as the definition in any state in which it wishes to sell beer.

The state definitions of beer might be simple. In Florida, for example, beer is "all brewed beverages containing malt." *See* Florida Statutes §563.01. In other states, the definition of beer includes an alcohol by volume limit. Any beers over that ABV limit are considered spirituous liquors. In Oregon, beer means "an alcoholic beverage obtained by the fermentation of grain that contains not more than 14 percent alcohol by volume." *See* Oregon Revised Statutes §471.001(6)(a)-(c). Alabama recently increased its ABV limit on beer from 6% to 13.9%, but only certain retailers and brewpubs may sell the higher alcohol beer. *See* the Code of Alabama §28-3-1 (as revised). Vermont's definition of beer is even more complicated: beer is "all fermented beverages of any name or description manufactured for sale from malt, wholly or in part, or from any substitute ... containing not less than one percent nor more than 16 percent of alcohol by volume at 60 degrees Fahrenheit. However, if such a beverage has an alcohol content of more than six percent and has a terminal specific gravity of less than 1.009, it shall be deemed to be a spirit and not a malt beverage." *See* Vermont Statutes Title 7, Chapter 1, §2(14).

Cider, Mead, and the States

The categorization of cider and mead in the states varies widely as well. In Florida, cider, because it is made from fruit, falls under the state's wine regulations. *See* Florida Statutes §564.01(1). Mead, on the other hand, does not neatly fall into any of the Florida defined alcoholic beverage categories. The question in Florida, and other states that do not include "other agricultural products" in the definition of wine, is: is mead a liquor by default? In Florida, if mead is treated as a spirituous liquor, only the state run ABC stores would be able to sell it.

In Oregon, the definition of beer specifically does not include cider "or an alcoholic beverage obtained primarily by fermentation of rice, such as sake." Wine in Oregon means "any fermented vinous liquor or fruit juice, or other fermented beverage fit for beverage purposes that is not a malt beverage [and also excluding cider], containing more than one-half of one percent of alcohol by volume and not more than 21 percent of alcohol by volume." *See* Oregon Revised Statutes §471.001(10). Mead would likely fall under this catch-all definition. Cider in Oregon has its own definition: "an alcoholic beverage made from the fermentation of the juice of apples or pears that contains not more than seven percent of alcohol by volume, including, but not limited to, flavored, sparkling or carbonated cider." *See* Oregon Revised Statutes §471.023.

In Vermont, wines are "all fermented beverages of any name or description manufactured or obtained for sale from the natural sugar content of fruits, or other agricultural product, containing sugar, the alcoholic content of which is not less than one percent nor more than 16 percent by volume at 60 degrees Fahrenheit." *See* Vermont Statutes Title 7, Chapter 1, §2(23). This definition of wine, by including "other agricultural product[s]" squarely puts cider and mead in the wine category.

Why Should I Care?

Beer, wine, and spirituous liquors, on both a federal level and a state level, are treated differently. Wineries often have more rights as to how they can sell their wine and to whom. Distilleries are often the most restricted category of manufacturer, and in the control states, only the state may sell a distillery's products. So, it is important to understand into which category an alcohol manufacturer's product will fall.

To simplify matters, this publication assumes that a brewery is producing beer, and not wine, nor a beer so high in alcohol content that it would be considered a spirituous liquor in some states. Several additional volumes could be written to deal with the regulations related to wines and high alcohol beers.

Question 5

How can a brewery sell beer? Or, what
separates a brewer from a bootlegger.

A brewery cannot legally sell beer in any state without first being licensed as a manufacturer or producer. Each state issues licenses for manufacturers (producers), wholesalers (distributors), importers, and retailers (vendors) of alcoholic beverages. The TTB must approve the business of any producer, wholesaler, or importer before that person or entity may make or sell any beer, or other alcoholic beverage. The approval process is aimed at ensuring that the governments can protect their tax revenue and keep the criminal element out of the alcohol industry.

Home Brewing

The federal government and most states have a specific exception to the licensing process for home brewers. There are exceptions, however. Alabama, Kentucky, and Mississippi do not have a home brew exception. Utah only recently passed a law allowing home brewing. In some states the laws surrounding home brewing are ambiguous at best (Iowa, Ohio, Oklahoma, Louisiana, Maine, and Nevada, among others).

In the states that do specifically allow residents to make their own beer, the licensing exception allows individuals to make beer, in certain quantities (usually tied to the federal limits), for personal and home consumption. The IRC contains the federal home brew exception, allowing for a certain amount of beer to be produced without the need to pay the beer excise taxes. The exception allows any adult ("an individual who has attained 18 years of age, or the minimum age ... established by law applicable in the locality...whichever is greater") to produce, without penalty of tax, for personal or family use, 200 gallons of beer per household each year (if there are 2 or more adults in a household), or 100 gallons of beer per household each year (if there is only one adult in the household). *See* §26 USC 5053(e) and §27 CFR 25.205. The state exceptions echo the federal language and often simply refer to the federal home brewing guidelines. The beer made under this exception is not subject to excise taxes on beer, but, it may not be sold.

The Brewery

Since brewers are in the *business* of making beer, this exception will not help them make money from their beer. A brewer, according to the IRS, is anyone who "brews beer...[and] produces beer for sale," except those people that brew beer for their own personal use. *See* §26 USC 5092 and §27 CFR 25.11. A brewery is the "land and buildings" described in the required notice of a brewer's intent to start a brewery. *See* §26 USC 5402(a). Generally, the buildings must be adjacent to each other, or, if there is a dividing medium, the buildings must abut it. *See* §26 USC 5402(a). A brewery may be used for "producing, packaging, and storing beer, cereal beverages containing less than one-half of one percent of alcohol by volume, vitamins, ice, malt, malt [syrup] and other byproducts and of soft drinks..." and for "processing spent grain, carbon dioxide, and yeast." *See* §26 USC 5411.

Commerce

A brewer selling the beer made at his or her brewery is engaged in commerce. This engagement in commerce is what makes the federal rules applicable to breweries in all states even if that beer never leaves the state. The sale of the beer does not need to cross state lines for the brewery to be engaged in commerce under the federal definition. *See* §27 USC 214(4). Even if you live in Puerto Rico, Guam, St. Croix, or the Midway Islands the federal regulations apply to you and your brewery.

The Licenses

The TTB does not distinguish between a package brewery and a brewpub (except in the form brewpubs and breweries have to submit monthly (see below)). Breweries and brewpubs both need to submit, and receive approval for, a Brewer's Notice with the TTB. Both are producing beer, and must pay excise taxes accordingly.

Most states, however, do distinguish between package breweries and brewpubs. The distinctions can be in the type of license issued, production limitations, or other requirements. The following state examples are provided solely to illustrate the variations on brewery and brewpub licenses states issue, and is not a guide to the state licensing structures.

States often have two different manufacturer licenses for breweries: one for a package brewery and another for a brewpub. In some states (Florida and Vermont, for example) a manufacturer license is issued to a brewpub in conjunction with a vendor's (or retailer's) license that allows the brewpub to sell beer to consumers on the brewpub premises. In other states (California, Michigan, and Alabama, for example) there is a specific brewpub license separate from a package brewery (manufacturer) license. Several states place gallon limits on how much beer a brewpub can produce each year. In, Florida, for example, a brewpub may only produce 10,000 kegs a year (or 5,000 barrels). *See* Florida Statutes §561.221.

To confuse the matter even more, there are other states that issue special microbrewery licenses. The term "microbrewery" usually refers to a package brewery that produces smaller amounts of beer annually. In microbrewery states, the microbrewery may have rights to sell directly to consumers as well as through the regular wholesale channels. The license cost is often less than a full manufacturer's license. The benefits of a microbrewery, however, are offset by the amount of beer a microbrewery may produce in one year. In Arizona, a microbrewery must produce more than 5,000 gallons (approximately 161 barrels) but less than 1.24 million gallons (approximately 40,000 barrels) annually. *See* Arizona Revised Statutes §4-205.08 (as amended). In New York, a microbrewery may not produce more than 60,000 barrels per year, or it will be subject to higher license fees and tax rates. *See* New York Alcoholic Beverage Control Law §56.

Question 6

What does a brewer need to do for a license? Or, the hoops a brew monkey has to jump through.

To obtain a license to manufacture and sell beer, a brewer needs to apply with the TTB as well as with the state in which he or she wishes to open a brewery in. Often, the brewer must be a resident of the state where the brewery will be opened. Before the brewer can even begin the applications, he or she needs to set up a corporate entity and obtain an EIN (or an employer identification number for tax payment purposes). There are as many filing requirements for every state as there are states. However, much of the information that a state alcohol control divisions require brewers to submit with their applications is the same information required by the TTB.

Brewer's Notice

Before making or selling beer, a brewer must file with the TTB, and receive approval for, a Brewer's Notice (TTB Form 5130.10). *See* §26 USC 5401(a). The Brewer's Notice requires information about the brewer, details about the intended business, the location, and the layout of the brewery premises. *See* §27 CFR 25.62. If the brewery will be a brewpub, the information regarding the "tavern" part of the premises must also be well detailed in the Brewer's Notice, as it is technically a variance from the normal brewery approvals. *See* §27 CFR 25.25.

Supplemental Information

The Brewer's Notice also requires supporting documentation regarding the business, including business organizational documents and a signature authority for anyone authorized to sign on behalf of the brewery. Brewers must also file a description of the land and the brewing premises, including the dimensions of the premises, what equipment will be used, and where the equipment will be located. *See* §27 CFR 25.65-68. A brewpub needs to be able to describe all procedures it will undertake to measure beer produced and sold for tax purposes, including, but not limited to, meters and tax termination tanks and their locations. *See* §27 CFR 25.25.

The supplemental documentation for a Brewer's Notice also requires a statement and documentation regarding the source of funds for the brewery (including copies of all loan documents, statements of any financial gifts, financial and bank account records), a statement regarding the legal description of the brewery premises (this can be obtained from the county recorder), the lease agreement for the premises (if there is one), and a statement describing the security (locks, alarm systems, etc.) at the brewery. Environmental and water quality forms also need to be filed with the Brewer's Notice (TTB Forms 5000.29 and 5000.30). The environmental and water quality forms require the brewer to describe how all solid and liquid waste will be monitored and disposed of, as well as any air pollution control equipment the brewery will use. The TTB includes a checklist of items that need to be filed with the Brewer's Notice (which can be found on-line at www.ttb.gov).

Typically, the TTB's approval process takes 95 days (once all the required documents are filed correctly). Each state has a different time line for issuing manufacturer or brewpub licenses, and has its own investigation process. Florida, will issue temporary licenses if it appears on the face of the application that there is no reason to deny the application. *See* Florida Statutes §561.181. The advantage of the temporary license is that the brewery may begin to produce beer as soon as it receives TTB approval, rather than waiting even longer for Florida's approval. Unfortunately, most states provide no such temporary license, and the applicant will have to wait to receive both the TTB's and the state alcohol control division's approval before it can even make any beer.

Along with the Brewer's Notice, each officer, director, member, partner, and any stockholder or member of 10% or more interest in the brewery needs to submit a Personnel Questionnaire listing any nicknames, aliases, and detailing any criminal history, especially if it involves any alcohol control laws or tax laws. Each Personnel Questionnaire requires that the applicant list bank and character references. The same rules apply in the states. Every person with an interest in the business of the brewery must submit a criminal history. This is how the governments keep the criminal element out of the alcohol business. Each state also requires that applicants be fingerprinted as part of the application process.

It is important to note that before a brewery receives its approval from the TTB and the state alcohol control division, the space for the brewery must be leased or purchased. Additionally, the equipment that will be used to make the beer (according to the information submitted in the Brewer's Notice) must either be ordered or already in its location at the brewery. But, the brewery cannot actually produce any beer for sale even if the space is rented and the equipment is in place. When negotiating for a commercial lease and equipment, it is important to make the contracts contingent upon the brewery receiving TTB approval and a license to operate from the state alcohol control division, as well as any necessary local approvals.

Changes to Brewer's Notice

If anything in the Brewers Notice changes at any time after the TTB approves the brewery for business, an amended Brewer's Notice must be filed with the TTB within 30 days of the change. Changes that require an amended Brewer's Notice include: the layout of the brewery (addition, deletion, or movement of equipment); alternation of the premises with another brewer; contract brewing to use extra capacity; additions or deletions of trade names; any changes in the location of the brewery; any changes in the stockholders, partners, or officers and directors in charge of management; and any changes to the signature authority of personnel. *See* §27 CFR 25.71-25.85 for details on when an Amended Brewer's Notice is required.

Again, this is true in the states as well, since they require the same information as the federal government does. Most states also require notice of any changes in the brewery's business within 30 days after the change. Filing an amended Brewer's Notice is very important. If there are any changes that the TTB has not been apprised of, the brewery is technically operating illegally, and making beer illegally, which will subject the brewery to a higher rate of tax (*see* below for more information on taxation), and the brewer will be subject to fines and other penalties.

If there is a change in ownership of the brewery, the new owner must qualify for a license first, before it can legally operate the brewery. The predecessor must also file all documents required for discontinuing the business. This is true on a federal level as well as a state level. New owners of an alcohol based business must independently qualify for a license. If the new owner has not independently qualified for a license, and the former owner has not filed its discontinuance paperwork, then both parties are in violation of the alcohol and beverage laws, and subject to fines and other penalties. If the brewery is operating during this time, the beer is being made illegally, and subject to higher tax rates.

Moral Character

The states have enacted laws to prohibit persons convicted of a felony or crime involving liquor laws, gambling, prostitution, or other crimes against morality from holding any interest (direct or indirect) in an alcohol license. Some states (Florida, for example) provide a lengthy list of which crimes will disqualify a person for a license, and what qualities constitute "good moral character." *See* Florida Statutes §561.15. Other states (Alabama, for example) simply state that licenses will be issued to responsible and reputable persons, rather than listing what will and will not cause a license to be denied. *See* Code of Alabama §28-3A-23(b). Some states even prevent a retailer (including brewpubs) from hiring anyone with a felony conviction.

How much does an alcohol license cost? Or,
the annual cost of being a professional brewer.

The opening of a brewery or brewpub has costs associated with it that are often not found in the opening of any other business. There are various costs associated with the licensing process alone, not to mention the costs associated with operating a brewery. Among the initial costs are the state license fees (there is no federal licensing fee), federal and state bond fees, and insurance costs particular to an alcohol beverage business. Of course, to even obtain federal approval and a state license, the brewery needs to have a leased space and equipment.

Each state charges a license fee for a manufacturer license. The state license fees can range from a few hundred dollars to tens of thousands of dollars, depending on the size and type of brewery. Some states also have administrative fees that are associated with any new license application.

Below are several examples of the approximate license fees for different states. The examples are provided only to illustrate the differences between fee structures among different states, and may not be used as a guide to the license fee structures of the states. License fees (including the amounts listed below) are subject to change at any given time.

In Alabama, the cost for an annual license for a brewery is $500, and $1,000 for a brewpub, with a $50 administrative fee for all new licenses. *See* Code of Alabama §§28-3A and 28-4A. In California, the application fee for a new brewery license is $100, with a $1,300 annual renewal fee. The new license fee for a brewpub, on the other hand, is $12,000 with an annual renewal fee of $600-$800 depending on the size of the city the brewpub serves.[2] In Colorado, the application fee is $1,025 and the fee for a brewery license is $150, and $825 for a brewpub.[3] Montana charges all new licensees a one time fee of $20,000 in addition to any renewal license fees.[4] Vermont charges breweries $250 annually, and brewpubs $450 annually.[5] As you can see, there is a wide range of fees that apply to the different licenses in different states.

Bonds

Another cost a brewery needs to be aware of is the cost of a federal bond. Some states also require bonds to be delivered to the alcohol control division. The purpose of the bonds is to ensure that the government is not cheated out of any tax money. If a brewery fails to pay its taxes, the government agency may "cash-in" the bond to cover any amounts owed by the brewery.

Each brewery must deposit with the TTB, along with its Brewer's Notice, a bond before starting any operations. *See* §26 USC 5401(a)-(b), §26 USC 5551(a) and §27 CFR 25.91-99. The penal sum (the amount) of the bond depends on the amount of beer the brewery will produce. Generally, if a brewer is filing semi-monthly tax returns (see details below on the tax payment structure), the penal amount of the bond will be 10% of the "maximum amount of tax...which the brewer will become liable to pay during a calendar year during the period of the bond on the beer..." *See* §27 CFR 25.93(a)(1). For brewers filing quarterly tax returns, the penal amount of the bond is 29% of the "maximum amount of tax...which the brewer will become liable to pay during a calendar year during the period of the bond on the beer..." *See* §27 CFR 25.93(a)(2). The minimum penal sum for the bond is $1,000. *See* §27 CFR 25.93(c). If a brewery is growing rapidly, and will likely be paying more tax liability, then, the brewery either has to pre-pay its taxes, or obtain a "strengthening bond" to cover the new penal sum. *See* §27 CFR 25.94.

---

2   *See* http://www.abc.ca.gov/permits/2009FeeSch.pdf.
3   *See* http://www.colorado.gov/cs/Satellite/Rev-Liquor/ LIQ/1209635769047.
4   *See* http://mt.gov/revenue/forbusinesses/alcohol.asp.
5   *See* http://liquorcontrol.vermont.gov/licensing/applications.html.

Bonds can be obtained through surety companies. Most large property and casualty insurance companies have surety departments. In order for a company to write a surety bond in the United States, it must be licensed by the insurance department of one or more states in which the surety conducts business. So, a good source of information on surety companies in the brewery's home state is often the state insurance department. Information about surety companies can also be obtained from The Surety & Fidelity Association of America (SFAA) www.surety.org.

The federal bond must remain active, or in-force, at all times the brewery is in business. *See* §26 USC 5551(a). Additionally, the bond must be renewed every 4 years, or a continuation certificate issued. *See* §26 USC 5401(b)(3) and §27 CFR 25.91(a). As a way to impose limitations on who can and cannot open a brewery, the TTB has the right to reject any bond if the applicant, or anyone owning a part of the business, has been convicted of any fraudulent non-compliance of the internal revenue code, or of any felony prohibiting the manufacture of alcoholic beverages. *See* §27 CFR 25.101(a). This is another method used by the TTB to ensure that criminals or persons with financially unstable businesses do not operate an alcoholic beverage business.

Some states require an additional alcohol tax bond to ensure the payment of state taxes. Others only require bonds from retailers and distributors, as they might be the entities required to pay excise and sales taxes. A brewpub in states that require bonds from retailers would likely need to provide a bond, as it is usually treated as a retailer for tax purposes. In all cases where a state bond is required, the bond must remain active or in-force during the entire time of the license, and must be renewed periodically.

Insurance Costs

Other costs particular to a brewery or brewpub to be aware of before even beginning brewery operations are certain insurance costs. Insurance costs range from location to location and depend on the business model of the brewery. There will be general liability, casualty, and dram shop (or liquor liability) insurance policies to purchase, and, depending on the size and number of employees, other insurance costs. If the brewery is a package brewery, some of the insurance costs may be less, depending on the location. On the other hand, if the premises are larger or the brewery has a tasting room, the insurance costs can go up. It is important to contact and work with a competent and licensed insurance agent when shopping for insurance for a brewery.

Can a licensed brewery sell beer to anyone?
Or, the long list of prohibitions.

Just because one has a license to brew and sell beer, does not entitle one to sell the beer to anyone and in any manner imaginable. Recall that the federal government and the states set up trade practice laws to deal with the perceived evils of the alcohol industry, such as tied houses. This is an area with a confusing maze of overlapping laws regulating what a brewer can and cannot do.

Trade practice restrictions on alcohol sales affect a brewery's business model. Understanding what the restrictions are will allow a brewer to plan a better business model from the beginning. The trade practice restrictions must also be taken into account when developing a financial analysis for the brewery.

FAA Act

The FAA Act controls alcoholic beverage trade practices on a federal level. The Act was the government's answer after the repeal of Prohibition to control the perceived problems pre-Prohibition and during Prohibition (over-consumption and organized crime, among others). The goals were to keep the criminal element out of the alcohol industry, and to protect consumers by regulating the formulation, labeling, advertising and marketing practices of alcoholic beverage businesses.

The FAA Act created a permit process to ensure that permits were kept out of the hands of persons with criminal convictions or with financially unstable businesses. Operators of any winery, distillery, wholesale, or import business need to apply for a federal permit. *See* §27 USC 204. Notice that breweries do not need to obtain a federal FAA Act permit, but, are still subject to the other rules and regulations of the FAA Act by default (more on this below). The trade practice provisions of the FAA Act are designed to prevent any wholesaler, producer, or importer from having control over a retailer to the exclusion of other suppliers.

Section 205, Title 27 of the USC, makes it unlawful for any person "engaged in business as a distiller, brewer, rectifier, blender, or other producer, or as an importer or wholesaler, of distilled spirits, wine, or malt beverages, or as a bottler, or warehouseman and bottler, of distilled spirits, directly or indirectly or through an affiliate..." to enter into exclusive outlet agreements, to have a "tied house," to commit commercial bribery, or to contract for consignment sales. We will deal with each of those issues separately below. It is important to remember that while the FAA Act does not require a brewer to obtain a basic permit (like wine or distilled spirits producers are required to do), the prohibitions contained in the FAA Act do apply to brewers and breweries by default. If there is a state law similar to the FAA Act governing the prohibited trade practice, then the federal rules apply. Similar law is defined very, very liberally, and in most cases the FAA Act rules apply in each state. *See* §§27 CFR 6.4(b), 8.4(b), 10.4(b), and 11.4(b).

Exclusionary Practices

Generally, the FAA Act prohibited trade practices are practices which "result in exclusion." This means that the trade practice either places (or has the potential to place) a trade buyer's (retailer's or wholesaler's) independence at risk, which results in the trade buyer purchasing less than it would have of a competitor's product. *See* §§ 27 CFR 6.151, 8.51, and 10.51. While some practices are considered exclusionary on the surface, the TTB will generally look at several factors in determining if the act constitutes exclusion, such as: whether the practice restricts or hampers the buyer's "free economic choice" when deciding what products to purchase; whether there is a continuing obligation for the buyer to purchase products from the industry member, or a commitment not to terminate the relationship with the industry member; whether the buyer has a continuing obligation to participate in the promotion of the industry member's products; and whether the practice is discriminatory and not offered to other buyers in the market. *See* §§ 27 CFR 6.153, 8.54, and 10.54.

The FAA Act restrictions (detailed below), as well as the restrictions applicable in the state a brewer wishes to set up shop, are important to be aware of when designing a business model, and when dealing with wholesaler and retailer contracts. At the state level, the restrictions are often included in the statutory license scheme. For example, the restrictions on a manufacturer's license will be detailed in the manufacturer license section. There may also be statutorily prohibited acts that are applicable to all manufacturers, wholesalers, importers, and retailers alike. When in doubt, every brewer should contact a competent licensed attorney in his or her state, as well as the TTB and the state licensing authority.

It is also important to remember that both parties will be responsible for a violation of the prohibited trade practices. A retailer cannot enter into these kinds of contracts nor can a wholesaler, manufacturer, or importer. Each will be guilty of a violation, and subject to penalties.

Exclusive Outlets

An exclusive outlet is, essentially, a contract between a manufacturer or wholesaler and a retailer that requires the retailer to purchase products only from that manufacturer or wholesaler. Exclusive outlets are prohibited. *See* §27 USC 205(a). These prohibited transactions only apply between industry members (wholesalers, producers, and importers) and retailers. A producer and a wholesaler can enter into such agreements. *See* §27 CFR 8.3. Generally, contracts that are entered into by a retailer under threat of physical or economic harm, or contracts that expressly require the prohibited act are considered to "result in exclusion" and violate the provisions of the FAA Act. *See* §27 CFR 8.52.

The prohibition on exclusive outlets not only applies to written contracts between an industry member and a retailer, but also to any situation that "has the effect of requiring [a] retailer to purchase [an alcoholic beverage product] from the industry member beyond a single sale transaction." *See* §27 CFR 8.22. A supply contract for one year or less that does not require the retailer to purchase a minimum quantity (such as an "as needed" contract) will not be a violation of the exclusive outlet prohibition. *See* §27 CFR 8.53.

Contracts that might have the effect of requiring a retailer to purchase exclusively from an industry member include: advertising contracts that (expressly or by implication) require the retailer to purchase the industry member's products; sales contracts that require for the period of the agreement that the retailer purchase a product or line of products exclusively from the industry member; or sales contracts that require the retailer to purchase a specific or minimum quantity during the period of the agreement. *See* §27 CFR 8.22.

A contract that requires a retailer to purchase beverages from the industry member beyond a single sales transaction will generally be under suspicion. For example, the following contract would be a violation of the exclusive outlet prohibition: a 12-month sales contract between a wholesaler and a retailer whereby the retailer agrees, because of a favorable price, to purchase all of its Bavarian wheat beers exclusively from that wholesaler.

The restriction on exclusive outlets also includes agreements that originate with a third party rather than the industry member (such as an organization that leases concession rights and is able to control the purchasing discussions of a retailer). The third party (such as a hotel) cannot require a retailer to purchase exclusively from one industry member.

Tied Houses

A "tied house" is a prohibited arrangement whereby an industry member induces a retailer to purchase products from that industry member to the exclusion of a competitor's products. This prohibition only applies between industry members and retailers, and not between industry members. So, a producer and a wholesaler can enter into such an arrangement. *See* §27 CFR 6.3.

Inducement includes:

- Holding an interest in any retailer's license (state, county, or municipal);
- Holding any interest in the real property used by a retailer (including holding a mortgage on the property or renting display space);
- Giving, renting, lending, or selling to the retailer supplies, signs, money, services, or any other thing of value (with a multitude of exceptions);
- Paying or crediting the retailer for any advertising;
- Guaranteeing any loan for a retailer;
- Extending credit to a retailer for more than 30 days after delivery; and
- Requiring a retailer to order a certain quota of products (including requiring a retailer to purchase one product in order to obtain another). *See* §27 CFR 6.21 and §27 USC 205(b). *See* §§ 27 CFR 6.25-6.72 for more details on the prohibited inducements.

All corporate officials, partners, employees, or any other representative of an industry member are prohibited from engaging in the unlawful inducements listed above. When it comes to the prohibition of providing anything of value to a retailer, even third party arrangements are prohibited. For example, if a manufacturer makes payments for advertising to a retailer association, whereby the retailer will benefit, that would be considered an illegal inducement. *See* §27 CFR 6.42.

Exceptions to the prohibition of giving anything of value to a retailer are found in Sections 6.81-102 of the CFRs, Title 27. Please see **Table 2** below for a description of what is allowed under the federal rules and regulations. Also keep in mind that a brewer needs to retain records (for three years) of all items furnished to any retailer. The records must show at least: the retailer's contact information, what was given to the retailer and when, the industry member's cost for the item, and what the retailer was charged for the item. *See* §27 CFR 6.81(b).

The FAA Act prohibits an industry member's interest in a retailer's business where the propriety ownership is partial. It does not prevent an industry member from "outright ownership of a retail business." *See* §27 CFR 6.27 and 6.33. This provision allows for different state licensing provisions which allow a manufacturer to self-distribute (i.e. to act as a retailer for its own products).

Commercial Bribery

The commercial bribery prohibition is applicable to transactions between industry members and trade buyers (whether they are a retailer or a wholesaler). *See* §27 CFR 10.3. The restriction prohibits industry members from giving anything of value to trade buyers in exchange for the buyer's purchase of the industry member's products, to the exclusion of a competitor's products. *See* §27 USC 205(c).

Any industry member's payment of money to a trade buyer (or by giving any bonus, premium, or other compensation) in return for the buyer agreeing to order alcoholic beverages from the industry member violates the commercial bribery prohibition. *See* §27 CFR 10.52. This includes any sales contests sponsored by an industry member that offers prizes to trade buyers. *See* §27 CFR 10.24.

Industry members may, however, give things of value to a wholesale *entity*, as long as those things of value are not passed down to the entity's employees, officers, or representatives. *See* §27 CFR 10.23. A producer or wholesaler can give a beer cooler to a retailer, for example, if the cooler is used in the business of the retailer. But, the industry member cannot give coolers to the retailer if those coolers will be distributed to the retailer's employees. Of course, there may be additional state restrictions (depending on the state) which prevent a producer from providing anything of value to a retailer, no matter what it is.

Consignment Sales

Prohibited consignment sales are sales made by an industry member to a retailer with the privilege or right of return. This prohibition applies between producers, importers, or wholesalers and trade buyers (wholesalers and retailers). So, a brewer may not sell his or her beer to a wholesaler or retailer on consignment, and a wholesaler cannot sell beer to a retailer on consignment. *See* §§ 27 USC 205(d) and 27 CFR 11.21.

Any arrangement where the "trade buyer is under no obligation to pay for [the alcoholic beverages] until they are sold by the trade buyer" constitutes a consignment sale. *See* §27 CFR 11.22. This also includes any arrangement for the exchange between the industry member and the trade buyer of one product for another different product (an exchange for equal quantities of the same product is not prohibited). *See* §27 CFR 11.23.

Returns of products that are unmarketable, where there are errors in the product delivered, or products that may no longer be legally sold, or when the trade buyer has terminated its business and returns products for a credit against indebtedness, where there is a change in the formulation of a product, or when a product is discontinued are not considered consignment sales. *See* §§ 27 CFR 11.31-11.39. Exchanges or returns due to overstocked, slow-moving, or seasonal products are not allowed (and will be considered consignment sales). *See* §§ 27 CFR 11.45-11.46.

State Restrictions

The states have similar trade practice laws to the FAA Act prohibiting exclusive outlets, tied houses, commercial bribery, and consignment sales. The state restrictions often do not use the same terms as the FAA Act. The state laws (whether contained in licensing sections or general prohibition sections) prohibit the same actions and types of contracts and arrangements that are prohibited by the FAA Act.

Each state prohibits a manufacturer or wholesaler from providing any item of value to a retailer. Suppliers (either manufacturers or wholesalers) are similarly prohibited from paying retailers for advertising or display space. The general prohibitions are then followed by numerous exceptions. California's tied house restrictions, for example, prohibit a supplier from providing anything of value to a retailer and from holding any ownership interest in a retailer's business. The prohibitions are then followed by almost 40 statutory exceptions. *See* California Business and Professions Code §§25500-25512.

The states, through the three-tier system, control who licensees may or may not sell products to. Typical three-tier states specifically prohibit manufacturers from selling directly to retailers or consumers (making an exception for brewpubs), and require that all retailers purchase their beer (and other alcoholic beverages) only from wholesalers. Some states have exceptions to this rule for wine, and some for beer. The following examples are provided only to illustrate how states legislate the three-tier system differently, and not as a guide to the state licensing systems.

In Massachusetts, a brewery located on a farm (as defined in the statutes) may act as a wholesaler and a retailer for the beer produced on that farm only. A farm brewery is allowed to sell its beer to consumers from the farm and directly to retailers. *See* Massachusetts General Laws §138-19C(f). In Florida, a package brewery may sell its beer directly to consumers from its brewery premises, if the brewery promotes "the tourist industry of the state." *See* Florida Statutes §561.221(2). The same brewery, however, may not sell its products directly to retailers. In California, one of the most liberal states when it comes to the three-tier system, breweries may sell directly wholesalers, to retailers, and to consumers (for both on and off premises consumption). *See* California Business & Professions Code §§ 23356 and 23357.

The most important exception to the three-tier rules is the brewpub exception. Brewpubs may produce beer and sell it directly to consumers from the brewpub premises in all states where brewpubs are allowed. There are differences in additional rights given to brewpubs. In some states a brewpub may also sell bottled beer or beer in growlers to be consumed away from its premises. In other states, it may only sell unpackaged beer on its premises.

Of course, knowing only the federal and a brewery's home state's laws is not the end of the story. If a brewer wants to start selling the brewery's beer in another state, he or she needs to become familiar with the limitations on manufacturers (as well as the excise tax structure) of the additional state(s) he or she wants to sell in. The brewer may be able to sell directly to consumers or retailers in his or her home state, but, in the new state he or she may only be allowed to sell through a wholesaler.

State Franchise Laws

To further complicate matters, many states have adopted detailed franchise laws governing the relationship between a manufacturer and its wholesaler or distributor. The purpose underlying the franchise laws was originally to check the power of suppliers over the middle (wholesaler) and lower (retailer) tiers. The stakeholders in the different tiers, however, have changed in form and power since these laws came into effect. While smaller wholesalers (who the franchise laws were initially intended to protect) have consolidated, the number of small craft breweries, wineries, and distilleries has grown (the TTB approved 224 new breweries in 2008 alone). The wholesale, middle, tier has additional protections, while the smaller manufacturers can no longer command the attention of the large distribution and retail houses.

State alcohol franchise laws often require a manufacturer to appoint an exclusive distributor for its products in a specific area for a specific time. This means that only that distributor may sell that product in that location for the time specified in the contract. A manufacturer is prohibited from allowing any other distributor to sell that brand of beer in that location.

Often, the franchise laws require notice to the state alcohol control division, and do not allow for a manufacturer to change distributors until the alcohol control division is notified with a document signed by both parties. Most of the franchise laws specify when a manufacturer may terminate its contract with the distributor. In most states with special franchise laws for the alcohol industry (Alabama, Connecticut, Florida, Massachusetts, North Carolina, and New Jersey are merely a few of the example states) a producer may not terminate a distributor without just cause, or good cause. Good cause often does not include a change of ownership in the manufacturer or the distributor, but does include a revocation of the distributor's license or the bankruptcy of a wholesaler. Most manufacturers and retailers in franchise states often find themselves required to deal with only one or two distributors in a given geographic area. It is very important to seek the advice of a competent licensed attorney to determine what is required for a distribution contract, and what the brewery may and may not do with respect to the distributor.

Question 9

What if I sell my brewery to a new owner? Or, why ordinary business transactions are more difficult in the alcohol industry.

Unlike other industries, if a brewery is sold to new ownership, the new owners need to be licensed before they can take over the brewery operations. All investors in the new ownership need to provide criminal histories, and financial information to both the TTB and the state alcohol control division. This means that if the deal closes before the new ownership is licensed with the state and the TTB, the new owners will not be able to legally produce beer.

Some states even continue to hold the prior brewer (license holder) responsible for all operations until the new owners are licensed. This could put the old brewer at risk for liability without the upside of sales for a brewery he or she no longer owns. It is important to work with a competent licensed attorney prior to any changes in ownership in a brewery, and to notify the TTB and the state alcohol control division long before the actual change takes place.

Even if there is only a small change in the ownership of the brewery, either new partners are added, or one partner is bought out, the TTB must be notified, through an amended Brewer's Notice. The state alcohol control division must also be notified of smaller changes in ownership of the brewery. Usually, notice of the changes must be filed with the TTB and the state alcohol control division within 30 days of the effective date of the change.

If the ownership of the brewery is going to be transferred to a new owner, the new owner must file an original notice, and be approved by the TTB, before beginning any operations, and the old brewer must file a notice stating that he or she is discontinuing operations. *See* §§ 27 CFR 25.72, 73 and 85. It is important to remember here, that the notice must be filed well in advance of the effective date of the change of ownership, otherwise the new owner of the business will not be able to operate until he or she is approved by the TTB.

The states also require that a new owner of a brewery independently qualify for a license. The new owner must apply for a license, and provide the same information required for the original application (criminal history, as well as financial information). Until the new owner is licensed, he or she cannot operate the brewery and cannot produce or sell beer. Some states, like Florida, may make it easier for a new owner to operate a brewery by allowing for a temporary license, provided that there is nothing on the face of the application that would result in a denial of the application. *See* Florida Statutes §561.331. Since the license approval process often takes several months, the acquisition documents should account for the operation of the brewery before the new owner is licensed. This could be done through a service agreement, or other methods.

Along with the state notification of a transfer, either of ownership, or location, administrative fees must be paid in each state for the transfer of the license either to another person or entity, or to another location. These fees can range from $30 (Florida, depending on the license held) to $2,000 (California, depending on the license held).

Question 10

How can I label my beer? Or, why your nude nymph label might be illegal.

The TTB generally regulates what can and cannot be on labels and advertising materials for alcoholic beverages. Labeling and advertising laws, rules, and regulations in the alcoholic beverage industry are often closely-tied. Labeling laws will often refer to advertising laws as to restricted statements, and vice versa.

The FAA Act outlines the general guidelines for alcoholic beverage labels and advertising. Labels include anything on any kind of container or promotional product, there are also federal keg and barrel requirements. All labels must be approved by the TTB before a product can be sold. The states require a copy of the TTB approval for any brand sold in that state.

There are also some states (Alabama and North Carolina, for example) that require all labels to also be approved by the state alcohol control division prior to its use. This means that a manufacturer making beer outside of those states must get its label approved by the state alcohol control division before selling its beer in that state (even if its label has already been approved by the TTB).

The federal regulations require that tanks in the brewery be marked with their capacity and a serial number. *See* §27 CFR 25.35. Kegs and barrels need to have the brewery's name and the address of where the beer is produced permanently marked on them. *See* §27 CFR 25.141(a). Short filled bottles of tax-paid beer (see below for information tax-paid beer), however, may be distributed to the brewery's employees without labels, as long as they are not for re-sale. *See* §27 CFR 25.142(f). All labels, for kegs, tap handles, barrels, and bottles must also go through the same label approval process described below. *See* §27 CFR 25.141(c) and §27 CFR 25.142(e).

Federal Label Requirements

Section 205(e), Title 27, of the USC states that a brewer cannot sell, ship, or deliver for sale any beer that is not marked, branded, or labeled in conformity with the federal laws. *See also* §27 CFR 7.20(b). The laws are intended to prevent the consumer from being deceived as to the nature, contents, and quantity of the product. To protect the consumer, the labeling laws prohibit false or misleading statements, disparaging statements about competitors, and anything that might confuse the consumer about the brand name or any endorsements. The laws also require certain information to be contained on any label.

Mandatory Statements

The following information **must** be included on the brand label itself and on any bottled beer (*See* §§ 27 CFR 7.22(a) and 27 CFR 25.142(a)):

- The brand name;
- The class of beverage (beer, ale, porter, stout, lager, etc.);
- The name and address of the brewery producing the beer;
- The net contents of the container (this must be stated in pints, quarts, gallons, or fractions thereof and fluid ounces, rather than in the metric system); and
- The alcohol content if the malt beverage contains any alcohol derived from added flavors or non-beverage ingredients.

The following information **must** be included on the brand label or on a separate label (back or front):

- The government health warning (see below);
- The name and address of importer (if imported);
- The name and address of the bottler or packer (if bottled or packed for the holder of an FAA Act permit or a retailer);
- The alcoholic content if required by state law (either marked as required by state law, or marked in percent "alcohol by volume" (the abbreviation "ABV" may not be used));
- A statement that the beverage contains FD&C Yellow No. 5 (if it does);

- A declaration of sulfites; and
- A declaration of aspartame. *See* §27 CFR 7.22(b).

Section 7.28, Title 27, of the CFRs, lists all the size and font size requirements for labels based on the size of the container.

Any food allergens may be disclosed on any label (for requirements and a list of allergens see §27 CFR 7.22a and 7.22b). *See also* §27 CFR 7.23-7.29 for additional label restrictions and requirements. The use of the word "organic" on any label (as well as any advertising materials - see below) is treated as "additional information" on labels. However, any use of the term "organic" on a malt beverage product must comply with the USDA's National Organic Program rules and regulations. These rules and regulations are beyond the scope of this publication. More information on organic labeling requirements can be obtained from the USDA's web site at www.usda.gov.

FDA Regulation

If a brewery is producing a gluten free beer it will be subject to the labeling requirements of the Federal Drug Administration (the "FDA"). Beers which are considered beer for excise tax purposes, but that are not malt beverages, are not subject to the TTB's labeling and advertising jurisdiction. This includes any fermented beverage brewed from a malt substitute such as sorghum or corn. *See* TTB Ruling 2008-3 and the FDA's Guidance. The FDA guidelines generally require that food products under its jurisdiction be truthfully and informatively labeled in accordance with the Federal Food, Drug, and Cosmetic Act, the Fair Packaging and Labeling Act, and the mirade of FDA regulations. These laws and regulations are beyond the scope of this publication. More information on the FDA's labeling requirements can be obtained from the FDA's web site at: http://www.fda.gov/Food/FoodIngredientsPackaging.

Class of Beer

One thing to note on the class of beverage required to be listed on a beer label, if the name of the class of beer includes a geographical name for a distinctive type of beer, it must also include the word "type" or "American," or the beer inside the container must actually conform to the type designated. The following are distinctive types of beer with geographical names that have not become generic: Dortmund, Dortmunder, Vienna, Wein, Weiner, Bavarian, Munich, Munchner, Salvator, Kulmbacher, Wurtzburger. *See* §27 CFR 7.24(f). For example, an American made beer must be called a "Wien Type" lager, or an "American Dortmunder." But, an American made beer may be called a "Pilsen," "Pilsener," or "Pilsner" without any further modification so long as the beer actually conforms to the type of beer. *See* §27 CFR 7.24(f) and (g). These rules on geographic names arose out of international intellectual property agreements, and preserve certain geographic names for products produced in those areas.

Government Health Warning

The other statutory federal labeling requirement is the government health warning which must be on all alcoholic beverage products distributed in, or imported into, the United States, including the District of Columbia, and all territories and possessions of the United States. *See* §27 USC 215 and §27 CFR 16.1-16.33.

> **GOVERNMENT WARNING:** (1) According to the Surgeon General, women should not drink alcoholic beverages during pregnancy because of the risk of birth defects. (2) Consumption of alcoholic beverages impairs your ability to drive a car or operate machinery, and may cause health problems.

The warning must be on the container label in a "conspicuous and prominent location," on a contrasting background, and the first two words must be in bold font and capitalized. *See* §27 CFR 16.22. There are additional requirements for font size depending on the container's size (contained in Section 16.22, Title 27, of the CFRs). The brewer cannot change the wording or add to the wording on the mandatory government health warning. This labeling requirement is not required if the beer is to be sold outside of the United States, or if it is intended for the armed forces of the United States. Also, the one thing that the states cannot mandate be placed on labels is any other health related statement. *See* §27 USC 216, §§ 27 CFR 16.31 and 16.32.

Prohibited Statements

Aside from the federal mandatory label requirements, there are certain statements that are not allowed to be included on any label (or other material accompanying the container, including coverings, cartons, cases, or other wrappers) sold to consumers in the United States. No label may contain any *(see* §27 CFR 7.29):

- False statements; statements that are disparaging of a competitor's products;
- Obscene or indecent statements, designs, or representations;
- Misleading statements, designs, or representations;

- A brand name of a living public figure or corporation (including graphic representations) that would lead a consumer to believe the figure or corporation endorses the product;
- Flags, seals, coats of arms, crests and other insignia;
- Statements that create a misleading impression that the beer contains distilled spirits;
- Any simulation or claim of a government stamp of approval or bond is prohibited;
- Any health-related statements; or
- Use of the words "strong," "full strength," "high proof," and other similar words, to describe the product itself. "Low alcohol," "reduced alcohol," and similar words may, however, be used on labels.

Interpretation of the label regulations shift with the agency's policies.

State Label Approval

As mentioned above, there are several states that require state label approval prior to the sale of the brand in that state. North Carolina and Alabama are examples of two states that require separate state review of all labels and advertisements, and just because a label has been approved by the TTB, does not mean that the same label will be approved by the alcohol control divisions of those states. Both Alabama and North Carolina's label and advertising regulations are combined in certain statutory sections, or the label regulations refer to the advertising restrictions. It is important to look at both the label and advertising laws and regulations of a state to determine what restrictions apply.

Alabama must approve all labels and advertising before its sale or dissemination in Alabama. No products may include anything which "might appeal to minors," anyone posed in an "immodest or sensuous manner," or any offensive language, among other things. *See* Alabama Administrative Code §§20-X-7-.01 and 20-X-8-.12. North Carolina also requires that its alcohol control division approve all labels and advertisements before they are sold or disseminated within the state. North Carolina prohibits all the things the federal government prohibits when it comes to labels or advertising (false or misleading statements, disparaging comments about competitors), but also prohibits images that are obscene, indecent, or "in bad taste," and anything that will induce someone under the age of 21 to drink. *See* North Carolina Administrative Code §04 02S.1005. The subjective state label requirements allow the state alcohol control division quite a bit of leeway in approving or denying a label.

Simply because a state does not require label approval before that brand may be sold in the state does not mean that the state does not have its own labeling requirements. Some states require that alcohol content be stated on the label; others prohibit the alcohol content from being stated on the label. Florida, for example, while it does not have to approve labels before they are sold in the state of Florida, does require that all brands must be registered with the state before they can be sold in Florida. In addition, all bottles of beer sold in Florida, must be marked with either the word "Florida," or "FL" in eight point font. A manufacturer can apply for an exception to this law, if it has a tracking system to identify the origination of the bottle (this is one of the reasons why bottles of beer in Florida often have brail-like dots at the bottom). *See* Florida Statutes §§ 563.045 and 563.06.

North Carolina, Alabama, and Florida are used for illustration purposes only, and may not be used as a guide to the state labeling requirements. There are other states that require label approval at a state level, and there are other states with different label requirements. It is important to understand a state's labeling (and advertising) laws before selling beer in that state, or advertising in that state. In practical terms, a manufacturer cannot create a label for a brand it will sell nationally without first investigating all of the state labeling requirements.

How do I apply for federal label approval? Or, a collection of certificates.

A certificate of label approval ("COLA") must be obtained for each brand before a brewery may bottle, pack, or remove any beer from the plant where it was produced. *See* §27 CFR 7.41. The COLA authorizes the bottling or packaging of that brand. When applying for the COLA, the TTB wants you to include a copy of any formula approvals (see below) or lab analysis of the beer in question.

The COLA is applied for by submitting Form 5100.31 to the TTB. *See* §27 CFR 13.21(a). The application may also be filed on-line, and the TTB encourages on-line applications. After receipt of the full application form, and all necessary supporting documentation, the TTB has 90 days to either approve or deny the application. *See* §27 CFR 13.21(b). If the application and label have been denied, there is an appeal process (the TTB will provide the applicant with a notice of denial that states the reasons why the label was denied). *See* §27 CFR 13.23-13.27.

Even after a COLA is issued, the TTB may, upon 45 days written notice to the COLA holder, revoke the certificate if it finds that the label at issue is not actually in compliance with the applicable laws or regulations. *See* §27 CFR

13.41-13.42. There is also an appeal process for a COLA holder to present arguments against revocation of its COLA, and to appeal any decision to subsequently revoke the label approval. *See* §27 CFR 13.43-13.45.

What can I include in my advertising? Or, why people can't appear to be having too much fun in beer adds.

The TTB also regulates all advertisements about alcoholic beverages in the United States, by enforcing the advertising sections of the FAA Act. *See* §§ 27 USC 205(f) and 27 CFR 7.50. The advertising regulations prohibit certain statements and make mandatory some information for all advertising and promotional materials. Of course, to complicate things further, there are state laws that also govern advertisements of alcoholic beverages within that particular state's borders. For the most part, the state laws and regulations follow the federal prohibitions, but not in all cases.

So, a brewer needs to be familiar with the federal advertising rules, as well as the advertising rules of his or her brewery's home state, and the rules of any other states in which he or she wishes to sell beer. As mentioned above, labeling and advertising laws and regulations are often closely-tied, and one must look at both sets of laws to determine what is and what is not allowed.

Federal Advertising Regulations

The FAA Act makes it unlawful to publish or disseminate any alcoholic beverage advertisement that deceives the consumer as to the nature, content, and identity of the product advertised. *See* §27 USC 205(f). This means that any false or misleading statements are prohibited, as are disparaging statements about competitors, and any obscene or indecent statements or images. It also requires certain information to be included in all adds or promotional materials.

Mandatory Statements

For all advertisements in the United States, the following mandatory statements must be included: the name and address of the brewer, bottler, packer, wholesaler, or importer responsible for the advertisement; the class of product (which must correspond to the statement of class of the product on the label). *See* §27 CFR 7.52. The mandatory statements must be legible, "in lettering or type size sufficient to be conspicuous and readily legible." *See* §27 CFR 7.53.

Prohibited Statements

The following is a list of prohibited statements for any advertisement of a beer product (*see* §27 CFR 7.54):

- False statements;
- Statements that are disparaging of a competitor's products;
- Obscene or indecent statements, designs, or representations;
- Misleading statements, designs, or representations;
- Misleading guarantees;
- Statements implying that the beer is brewed under the laws of any state or municipal authority;
- Any statement implying governmental supervision of the product;
- Statements that create a misleading impression that the beer contains distilled spirits;
- Any statement that is inconsistent with the label of the product;
- Any use of the words "strong," "full strength," "high proof," and other similar words;
- Health related statements;
- Any statement that might create a confusion of brands among consumers;
- Any flags, seals, coats of arms, crests, or other insignia of the United States, the armed forces, organization, family, or individual; or
- Any other deceptive statements or techniques (including subliminal techniques).

The federal advertising laws and regulations apply to all advertising material, including coasters and other promotional giveaways. Advertisements do not need to be pre-approved by the TTB.

Federal Trade Commission

There is one more layer of federal regulation on alcoholic beverage advertisements: the Federal Trade Commission (the "FTC"). The FTC's function is to protect consumers in the United States by regulating unfair and deceptive advertising and trade practices. The FTC's regulation is supplemental to the TTB's regulation, rather than a replacement for it; both regulate any false or misleading statements in advertising. The FTC has independent authority to investigate violations, require documentation, as well as issue subpoenas in an investigation.

The FTC takes the position that advertisements that may encourage underage drinking or irresponsible behavior are prohibited by the FTC Act. Whether this kind of marketing is unfair or deceptive is another issue, but no alcohol advertiser has challenged the FTC's position. Some industries have developed voluntary industry advertising codes. The Brewer's Association, as well as the Beer Institute both have industry advertising codes, and self regulate their members for compliance.[6,7]

Beer Industry Advertising Codes

Some of the items in the beer industry advertising codes include: that advertisements should not condone driving and drinking, boating and drinking, or excessive consumption; that the advertiser must reasonably believe that its audience will contain at least 70% persons above the legal drinking age; and that web sites should have age verification mechanisms. The 70% placement standard is somewhat difficult to determine in print or web based advertising (the Nielsen Media Research is useful for determining the audience for the television adds). The FTC looks to these industry standards when enforcing the unfair and deceptive trade practices regulations.

One of the problems with the FTC is that you have to wait until they come after you for a violation. The FTC will not issue opinions or clear advertisements the way the TTB will. In the past, their investigations of alcohol manufacturers have not resulted in fines, but in consent orders. Consent orders between the FTC and the advertiser require the advertiser to agree for a certain amount of time not to include certain things in its advertising materials.

---

6   The Brewer's Association Advertising Code can be found at:
     http://www.beertown.org/craftbrewing/pdf/MarketingCode.pdf.

7   The Beer Institute's Advertising Code can be found at:
     http://www.beerinstitute.org/BeerInstitute/files/ccLibraryFiles/
     Filename/000000000384/2006ADCODE.pdf.

State Advertising Regulations

Also remember that the states have advertising requirements and restrictions that may include additional prohibited statements or images. Often, any additional prohibited statements or images are couched in vague terms, like North Carolina's prohibition against anything that might induce anyone under the age of 21 to drink. Some states (such as Alabama and North Carolina, among others) require that all advertisements, regardless of the form, be pre-approved by the state alcohol control division before their dissemination in that state. Some states have restrictions on when and where alcoholic beverage advertisements can be made (i.e. radio, billboard, and television restrictions). In practical terms, a supplier cannot run a national add campaign without addressing the states' idiosyncrasies.

Question 13

Can I make any kind of beer, any way I want?
Or, why innovative beers can cause more headaches.

The TTB must approve certain formulas for beer before it can be produced for sale. If a brewery will produce its beer in a traditional process, it does not need to obtain formula approval from the TTB. Non-traditional processes for which TTB approval must be sought include: "removal of any volume of water from beer, filtration of beer to substantially change the color, flavor, or character, separation of beer into different components, reverse osmosis, concentration of beer, and ion exchange treatments." *See* §27 CFR 25.55(a)(1)(i). The brewer will not need to file a formula for any process that includes pasteurization, filtration prior to bottling, filtration in lieu of pasteurization, centrifuging for clarity, lagering, carbonation, and blending. *See* §27 CFR 25.55(a)(1)(ii). A TTB formula approval must also be obtained for any fermented product to which flavors, non-beverage ingredients, coloring, natural or artificial flavors, fruit, fruit juice, fruit concentrate, herbs, spices, honey, maple syrup, or any other food materials are added. Sake and sparkling sake also require TTB formula approval. *See* §27 CFR 25.55(a).

A separate formula must be filed and approved for each different product the brewer intends to produce in a non-traditional manner. *See* §27 CFR 25.55(a). The formula must be filed in writing, and list each separate ingredient, and the quantity (or range of quantities) used, the process used to produce the beer, and the alcohol content. *See* §27 CFR 25.57. If a brewer is using any flavorings containing alcohol, there are additional formula disclosure require-ments. If the formula provided to the TTB is not specific enough (if the ranges of quantities of ingredients is too wide, for example) the TTB will ask for more specificity before it approves the formula.

Superseding and new formulas must be filed and approved (before production and sale) if: (1) a new product is created, (2) new ingredients are added to (or ingredients are deleted from) an existing formula, (3) the quantities or range of quantities of an ingredient is changed, or (4) the process is changed. *See* §27 CFR 25.58.

Where can I set up my brewery? Or, watch out for schools and churches.

Most states, as well as counties and municipalities, have restrictions on where a brewery may be opened. These restrictions may state, for example, that a brewery (or any alcoholic beverage business) may not be operated within a certain distance of a school or church. The restrictions may be contained in the alcohol laws of that state, or in the state, county, or municipality zoning ordinances. Below are several examples of some statewide restrictions on where an alcohol based business may be located. The examples are provided to illustrate how different states deal with the restrictions, and may not be used as a guide to the state regulations on where a brewery may be located.

Garage Brews

The federal rules prohibit a brewery in a dwelling house. So, you cannot brew and sell out of your home. Brewing out of a garage or basement is a grey area. Depending on what the state allows, the TTB may, or may not, approve a garage or basement brewery. Certainly some breweries have been approved for basement or garage breweries in the past (New Belgium and Rock Art). But, in order for the basement or garage to be approved several requirements must first be met.

First, the basement or garage must be zoned for the brewery use. This usually means that the area must be zoned for industrial or light industrial uses (depending on the municipality). In some cases it is possible to get a variance from the zoning restrictions. In most cases, however, if an area is zoned as residential, it is highly unlikely that a variance for a brewery will be granted.

Second, the basement or garage must typically either be detached from the house or have a separate entrance. Recall that a brewery needs to submit a diagram of the property (showing where the brewery is located on the property and its relation to the house) along with the Brewer's Notice. If the garage is attached to the home, the TTB has stated that it is unlikely that it will approve the use.

Schools and Churches

When looking at locations for a brewery, it is important to consider local zoning issues. First, be familiar with what kind of use a brewery is considered. In some localities it might be considered an industrial use, in others, merely a commercial use. Second, be familiar with the approved zoning for the location you are interested in. If necessary, obtain a variance before beginning the application process. The TTB and state alcohol control division are unlikely to approve a brewery application if the location is not properly zoned for a brewery.

In Arizona, no alcohol based business may be located within 300 feet of a church, school, or recreational area. See Arizona Revised Statutes §4-207. In Colorado, a brewery may not be located within 500 feet of a school or college. See Colorado Code of Regulations §47-326. Alabama has an even stricter statewide restriction, with some exceptions for larger cities: no alcohol based business may be located within one mile of a school or charitable institution (including churches), unless it is within 400 feet of a courthouse. See Code of Alabama §28-3-17.

When looking for a location to open a brewery, it is important to work with competent and licensed real estate agent and attorney in that state to determine any location restrictions and obtain a variance if necessary. The last thing you want is to get into a commercial lease and realize that you may not open a brewery there. Or, that you may produce beer, but cannot open a tasting room on that location. Make sure that you plan your business from the beginning and that your location allows for all aspects of your plan before committing.

What kinds of taxes do I need to pay? Or, why alcohol manufacturing is more expensive than making toys.

As a business, any brewery or brewpub will have to pay its income taxes to the state and the federal government. But, that is not all. To control consumption and to raise revenue, the federal government and the states have placed excise taxes on alcoholic beverages.

On top of the excise taxes, there are state and local sales taxes which must be collected from consumers who purchase alcoholic beverages and paid to the state, county, or municipality. The sales tax is usually calculated on the retail value of the product, before other taxes are included. In some states (Florida, for example) the taxes are calculated on the total amount of the sale (including the excise tax), rather than on the retail price before taxes.

This section focuses on alcohol excise taxes. Brewers should always seek the advice of competent licensed financial professionals and attorneys to determine their overall tax liability. The TTB's tax collection division can be a great resource when calculating a brewery's federal excise tax liabilities. The information necessary to determine the federal excise tax liability will also be the same information necessary to determine any state excise tax liability.

Federal Excise Tax

The federal excise tax is $18 per barrel, or percentage thereof (a barrel, for federal tax collection purposes, contains 31 gallons). See §26 USC 5051(a)(1). The base amount of the federal beer tax is reduced if the brewery produces less than 2,000,000 barrels a year. So, for smaller breweries, the tax is $7 per barrel for the first 60,000 barrels, and then $18 per barrel for each barrel over 60,000. See §26 USC 5051(a)(2)(A). To qualify for the reduced rate of tax on beer, a brewery needs to file a notice with the TTB (either in the original Brewer's Notice, or in any subsequent amended Brewer's Notices). See §27 CFR 25.167.

If a brewery is not in compliance with all the federal laws, rules, and regulations with respect to its operations (including filing amended notices with the TTB if any changes in the ownership or operation of the brewery occur), and it continues to produce beer, that beer is illegally produced beer. Beer produced illegally is taxed at the $18 a barrel rate, and is also due and payable as soon as it is produced (not when it is removed from the brewery premises as described below). See §26 USC 5054(a)(3). Of course, the brewery may also incur fines and other penalties for producing beer illegally.

Removed Beer

The federal excise tax must be calculated on all beer that is produced and removed from the brewery for consumption or sale. See §26 USC 5054(a)(1). "Removed for consumption or sale" means either the "sale and transfer of possession of beer for consumption at the brewery," or any "removal of beer from the brewery." See §27 CFR 25.11. It does not include beer that is removed (1) for export outside the United States, (2) because it is sour or otherwise damaged, (3) for laboratory analysis, (4) for research and development and testing, (5) for use as distilling material in a distilled spirits plant, (6) for use by foreign embassies if removed to a customs warehouse, (7) for destruction, (8) for certain vessels and aircraft, and (9) for delivery to another brewery owned by the same brewer. See §§ 26 USC 5053(a)-(d), (f)-(i) and 5414 and §27 CFR 25.191-225.

According to the TTB general practices, beer consumed in tasting rooms may or may not be subject to the excise tax. If the tasting room is on the brewery premises, and consumers are not charged at all (including any parking charges or fees for tasting glasses), then the beer can be consumed on premises, without the payment of tax. If, however, consumers are charged any fees, the brewery must pay the excise tax on all beer served in the tasting room. Brewers should contact the TTB to determine when and if the beer served in their tasting rooms will be subject to federal excise tax liability.

The Internal Revenue Service ("IRS") cares about *when* beer is removed from a brewery's premises, so it can determine how much the brewery owes in taxes. The IRS also cares about *how* the beer is removed: it must only be in "hogsheads, packages, and similar containers, marked, branded, or labeled" as required by federal regulations. *See* §26 USC 5412. Other similar packages are: bottles, cans, kegs, barrels, or other original consumer containers. §26 USC 5416. Beer can also be removed through pipelines to contiguous distilled spirits plants. *See* §26 USC 5412.

Tax Refunds

Thankfully, if beer is returned, destroyed, received at a distilled spirits plant, or exported, the brewery can receive a refund of any tax paid on those barrels if it files the refund claim within six months after such return or loss. *See* §§ 26 USC 5056 and 5062, *see also* §§ 27 CFR 25.281-282. If a brewery does not file the refund claim in the time allotted (six months), it will not receive a refund of any taxes paid on destroyed, returned, or exported beer.

Destruction Of Beer

There are also rules for when and how a brewer can destroy beer. If the brewer will destroy the beer on the brewery site before it is officially removed from the brewery, it may be destroyed without prior notice to the TTB (although, the quantities of destroyed beer must still be recorded). However, if the beer needs to be destroyed at a location other than the brewery site once the beer has been removed from the brewery, the brewer needs to provide the TTB with 12 days prior written notice regarding the particulars of any destruction (quantities, manner, dates, and method) of the destruction. *See* §27 CFR 25.222-225. See CFR Section 25.283 for a list of requirements when filing for a tax refund on lost, destroyed, or returned beer.

Tax Returns

A brewery pays the federal excise tax by filing a return along with a check in the amount of its tax liability. The tax needs to be paid and the return filed by the 14th day after the last day of the preceding period. *See* §§ 26 USC 5061(a)-(d). Larger breweries need to pay and file the return every two weeks. Breweries that expect to have less than a $50,000 tax liability for the year, and had less than $50,000 tax liability the year before, for all beer removed, can file the return and pay their tax quarterly. *See* §26 USC 5061(d)(4)(A) and §27 CFR 25.164(c)(3). Remember that in order to be able to file the deferred tax return, a brewery filing quarterly, needs to calculate it's bond amount at 29% of its estimated yearly tax liability (*see* the How Much Does an Alcohol License Cost Section above for more information in the federal bonds required). Breweries can file their returns and pay their taxes electronically. If any taxes are not paid timely, or the penal sum of a brewery's bond is not sufficient to cover its tax liability, however, the brewery must prepay its taxes either in cash, by certified check, or money order. *See* §27 CFR 25.173-175.

In a contract brewing situation (*see* the What About Alternative Brewing Situations Section below for more details), a brewer may obtain his or her beer from another brewer, in containers marked with his brand and address. The taxes on that beer must be paid by the producer of the beer. *See* §26 USC 5413. The contracting brewer is almost functioning as a wholesaler or retailer at that point.

State Excise Taxes

State excise taxes on alcohol range from $0.02 per gallon (Wyoming) to $1.07 per gallon (Alaska). The Center for Science in the Public Interest publishes a breakdown of state excise and sales taxes.[8] Generally, the excise taxes must be paid monthly to the state. In some states, counties or municipalities may also charge excise taxes on alcoholic beverages.

Generally, in strict three-tier states the wholesaler is responsible for calculating, charging, paying to the state, and keeping adequate records of the excise taxes. But, this may not always be the case depending on the state. Retailers are responsible for collecting sales taxes from consumers, and paying it to the state, as well as keeping adequate records of sales and taxes owed. Brewpubs, since they are selling to consumers, must calculate, charge, collect, and keep records of both the excise tax and the sales tax.

Manufacturers that sell their products to wholesalers, retailers, or consumers in other states will be responsible for paying the applicable excise and sales taxes in that state. For example, a Florida brewery that wishes to sell its beer in Colorado will not need to pay the Florida excise and sales taxes on beer removed from its brewery to be sold in Colorado, but will have to pay the excise and sales taxes applicable in Colorado.

---

8   *See* http://cspinet.org/new/pdf/state_rank--jan_2009.pdf.

What information do I need to keep track of during operations? Or, why large file cabinets are good things.

Before starting the brewery operations, it is helpful to understand what kind of information brewers are required to provide to the state and the TTB on a monthly basis. Knowing this from the beginning can help produce monthly operations reports much more quickly. The required operations reports of a brewery go hand-in-hand with the calculation of a brewery's tax liability.

Report of Operations

A brewery calculates and pays its federal excise tax on the basis of the information contained in the brewery's monthly report (the Brewer's Report of Operations, TTB Form 5130.9, and the brewpub Report of Operations, TTB Form 5130.26). The Report of Operations must be filed with the TTB along with the brewery's tax return. If a brewery is on a quarterly tax payment schedule, it will only need to fill out and file the Report of Operations quarterly. See §27 CFR 25.297(b). Generally, the information required in the federal Report of Operations is the same information required to report to the state alcohol control divisions on a monthly basis.

Records

Brewers must keep records of all individual transactions, all data used in compiling any TTB or tax form, all notices, all reports, any approved applications, daily records of operations (including all beer produced, racked, bottled, each kind and quantity of material received, removed and for what reasons), all ballings of wort produced, unsalable beer, and all other documents relating to the operations of the brewery. *See* §27 CFR 25.291-296. Brewers must also keep records regarding all yeast removed from the brewery, and all malt syrup, wort, and any other materials removed from the brewery. The records must show the date, quantity, and to where the material was removed. *See* §27 CFR 25.251-252. See **Table 3** for a break down of all items that a brewery will need to keep track of in order to complete the Report of Operations.

Inventories

In addition to keeping these various records, brewers need to complete a physical inventory each month. The inventory reports need to be signed by the person who actually performed the inventory, and filed with the TTB monthly. Each inventory report needs to show: the date the inventory was taken, the quantity of beer on hand, losses, gains, and any shortages. *See* §27 CFR 25.294.

Time Limits

A brewer must maintain all records for three years. *See* §27 CFR 25.300(c). The states also require that brewers keep similar records to those required by the TTB, for three years as well. Also, keep in mind that, the TTB has the right to install meters, tanks, or any other measuring device "for the purpose of protecting revenue." *See* §26 USC 5552. The cost of any such installations and maintaining the equipment will be the brewer's responsibility.

TTB Rights

The TTB, as well as the state alcohol control divisions, have the right of entry and examination of any brewery or brewpub during normal business hours. The TTB officers, and state alcohol control division officers, have the right to inspect the premises, all aspects of the brewing operations, and all the brewery's records. *See* §27 CFR 25.51. The TTB also has the right at any time to request from any brewery or brewpub samples of any beer or other alcoholic beverages produced as well as any materials used in the process. *See* §27 CFR 25.53.

What about alternative brewing situations?

Or, how to make alternate brewing and contract brewing arrangements work with the TTB.

Starting with your own equipment in a leased space or garage (if the state allows this) is not the only way to start a low budget brewery. Brewers can contract with a brewery that has extra capacity to use that brewery's space and equipment (this is known as an alternating proprietorship). Alternating proprietorships (an arrangement in which two or more people take turns using the premises of one brewery) are different from contract brewing arrangements (an arrangement in which one person pays a brewing company, the "contract brewer," to produce beer for him or her). In an alternating proprietorship arrangement, the proprietor of an existing brewery (the "host brewer") generally rents space and equipment to a new "tenant brewer."

Alternate Proprietorships

The TTB will allow requests for an alternate method of operation as a variance to the general practices. In this situation each brewer must separately qualify with the TTB. The tenant brewer must produce its own beer, hold title to all the brewing ingredients and beer at all stages of the brewing process, and must keep its own records, labels, certificates of label approval, submit its own bond to the TTB, and pay all of its own taxes. The tenant brewer's beer must be separate and identifiable from the beer of the host brewer, or any other tenant brewer on the premises, at all stages (including before, during and after fermentation, during cellar storage, and as finished beer after production and before removal).

The TTB also requires that the tenant brewer submit a business plan (showing future development plans for the brewery) with its Brewer's Notice. A copy of the entire agreement with the host brewery must also be submitted to the TTB with the Brewer's Notice, and the host brewery must submit an amended Brewer's Notice. More information on the TTB's requirements and treatment for alternating proprietorships can be found in the TTB's Circular 2005-2, available on its web site at www.ttb.gov.

The TTB will not allow arrangements that are designed to split up a larger brewery into smaller breweries to qualify for the reduced tax rate. It will look to see if the labels, brand names, or trademarks of the host and tenant brewers are the same, or substantially similar. The TTB will not approve alternation agreements where the tenant brewer's access to the brewery premises is restricted.

To complicate matters, the state might also have its own laws, rules, and regulations regarding the alternation of a brewery. Or, the state might not have encountered the alternative brewing arrangement before, and does not know how to deal with it. In all cases, it is imperative for brewers to check with their state alcohol control division and a competent licensed attorney before entering into any alternation arrangement.

Contract Brewing

A contract brewing arrangement is another alternative brewing situation to bring a brewery's costs down. Contract brewing is viewed by the TTB as a purely business arrangement whereby one person (either a wholesaler, retailer, or brewer) pays the contract brewer to make beer for him or her. The contract brewer is entirely responsible for producing the beer, keeping appropriate brewery records, labeling the beer with its name and address, obtaining the necessary COLAs, and paying all taxes for the removal of the beer from the brewery. The contract brewer retains title to all the ingredients and the beer, at least until the beer is tax-paid or removed from the brewery.

In a contract brewing situation, the purchasing brewer may supply the producing brewer with barrels and kegs marked with the purchasing brewer's information and brand, and purchase finished beer from the producing brewer. The producing brewer is responsible for paying all taxes associated with the production of beer. *See* §27 CFR 25.231(a). The purchasing brewer, however, cannot purchase beer (for which the producing brewer has paid tax) in bottles or cans with the purchasing brewer's information and brand marked on them. *See* §27 CFR 25.231(b). If a brewer purchases beer from a producing brewer for resale, he or she is required to obtain a wholesaler's or importer's basic permit under the FAA Act. *See* §27 CFR 25.232.

Again, the states may have their own laws, rules and regulations pertaining to contract brewing situations. Many states do not have explicit laws, rules, or guidelines for dealing with alternative brewing situations. Brewers should contact their state alcohol control division and a competent licensed attorney before entering into any contract brewing arrangement.

Question 18

How do I put it all together? Or, the steps to setting up a brewery or brewpub.

The first formal step in the process to open a brewery is filing the Brewer's Notice with the TTB, along with all the required supplemental information and documentation.

Before the Brewer's Notice may be filed, however, the brewer needs to: 1) register a corporate entity with his or her home state and obtain an EIN for tax payment purposes; 2) have a business plan created for the type of brewery he or she wishes to open; 3) have financing squared away; 4) have a space leased; and 5) either have on hand, or have ordered, the equipment necessary to produce the beer.

Once the TTB approves the Brewer's Notice, the brewer should apply for a state license. In some cases these applications can be filed concurrently. The state license will need to be renewed annually.

After the brewery is licensed, it will need to apply for label and formula (if necessary) approval from the TTB. Depending on the state the brewery is set up in, or the states it wishes to sell beer in, it may also need to apply for additional label approval.

The brewery will most likely also need to work, and contract, with a wholesaler if it is a package brewery. The requirements to sell through a wholesaler will vary from state to state.

If there are any changes to the brewery, either in the ownership, or the layout, the brewer will need to notify the TTB and the brewery's state alcohol control division.

The brewery will need to keep detailed records of all beer produced, packaged, and sold. A monthly inventory must be taken. The brewery will need to file monthly reports, tax returns, and tax payments with the TTB (unless it is on a quarterly tax schedule) and the state alcohol control division. In addition, the brewery must keep all records for three years.

What other issues should I worry about? Or
why the age of 21 is like magic.

National Minimum Drinking Age

Any brewery or brewpub selling beer to consumers needs to know and understand its state's laws regarding the minimum drinking age. The National
Minimum Drinking Age Act requires the states to legislate a minimum drinking
age of 21, and the Federal Aid Highway Act subjects any state that fails to
legislate the minimum drinking age to a decrease in its annual federal highway
funds. The states have reacted differently to the federal minimum drinking age
requirement.

Some states make possession, consumption, purchase, and furnishing alcoholic beverages to under aged persons illegal (Alabama, Arizona, New Hampshire, and Pennsylvania, among others). Some states prohibit possession,
purchase, and furnishing alcohol to under aged persons, but not consumption
(California, Florida, Georgia, Nevada, and New Mexico, among others). Others provide for family exceptions to the prohibitions making it legal to possess
and consume alcohol around one's parents or guardians (Alaska, Colorado
Idaho, New York, Oregon, Ohio, Texas, and Wisconsin, among others). And,
still others have family and location (in the home) exceptions to the prohibitions (Alaska, Colorado, New Mexico, and Minnesota, among others).

Florida's legislators even went so far as to enact the 21 year-old drinking age under protest. Florida's minimum drinking age law provides that "in the event that a federal court of last resort determines that it is unconstitutional for the Federal Government to withhold transportation funds from the state because the legal age of the sale, consumption, or possession of alcoholic beverages is under 21 years of age or if federal legislation is enacted to allow the drinking age to be lowered or modified from 21 years of age, it is the intent of the Legislature that [the age restrictions revert back to 18 years of age]." *See* Florida Statutes §§562.11.

Responsible Vendors

Some states have set up "responsible vendor programs," designed to educate vendors and their employees on the drinking laws. Alabama, California, Colorado, Florida, Louisiana, Oregon, and Tennessee, among others, have all set up some sort of responsible vendor training and certification program. Typically the programs are voluntary prevention and education programs for retail licensees, their employees, and agents (this includes any manufacturer with a license to serve beer, either in a tap room or as a brewpub, to the public). In certain states certification as a responsible vendor, in some circumstances, will prevent the licensee from having its license suspended if its employee (who has been through the training) accidentally serves and under aged person.

Employees

The minimum drinking age also plays a role in who a brewery can and cannot hire. If an under aged person cannot even possess alcoholic beverages in a given state, then it might follow that a brewery or brewpub cannot hire that person. Even states that make the possession of alcohol by under aged persons illegal often have exceptions for hiring workers. Sometimes the state laws allow a brewpub to hire persons 18 years and older as servers (California, Florida, Louisiana, Oregon, Virginia, among others). In a few states (such as Nevada and Utah) servers must be 21 years of age or older. In other states, the minimum age for a server might be 19 and older (Arizona, Alabama, Idaho, and Ohio, among others).

Package breweries that sell directly to consumers from their licensed premises, must, in a few states, employ associates over the age of 21 (Colorado, New Mexico, and Utah, among others). While others specifically allow anyone over the age of 15 to sell beer for off-premises consumption (Arizona, Texas, and Nevada), many do not specify a minimum age for sale of beer for off-premises consumption (like California, Florida, and New York, among others).

The state examples above have been provided only to illustrate how many legal variations the states created to deal with the minimum drinking age. The examples are not a guide to the state minimum drinking age laws. Once again, it is important that every brewery seek the advice of a competent licensed attorney to determine who it can and cannot serve and hire. A good breakdown of what states do and do not allow with respect to the minimum drinking age can be found at the Alcohol Policy Information System's web site: http://alcoholpolicy.niaaa.nih.gov.

Dram Shop Liability

Another related serving issue for breweries with tasting rooms and brewpubs is dram shop (liquor) liability, or, when the brewery may become liable in a civil action (rather than criminally liable, or liable for administrative penalties) for the actions of one of its patrons. If, for example, the brewery serves the patron and he crashes into a school bus full of puppies on the way home. Is the brewery liable for damages to the bus and puppies? Each state has different laws, rules and regulations for when the brewery might be liable for another's actions. The various laws have often been heavily litigated in the civil courts of each state. Dram shop liability issues are very complicated and beyond the scope of this publication. It is very important for brewers to know their states' laws regarding this issue, and to work with a qualified insurance company to obtain adequate insurance against this kind of liability.

Question 20

Are there some areas where I cannot sell beer? Or, where an Orange Dodge Charger might be needed.

There are states in the United States that allow counties to have "location options," meaning that the counties can choose to be dry or wet counties. Often in dry counties the manufacture, sale, consumption, and even possession of alcoholic beverages are illegal. As we have seen before, each state has its own variety of dry counties. In Alabama, absolutely no alcohol is permitted in dry counties. In Florida, however, even in dry counties, beer that is 6% ABV or less can be sold, consumed, and possessed. *See* Florida Statutes §§567 and 568. Typically, in states with dry counties, one is permitted to transport alcoholic beverages through a dry county as long as the beverage is not delivered, opened, or consumed in that dry county.

Question 21

Are there other things to worry about when selling beer to consumers? Or, when the clock strikes midnight.

To control consumption, most states have legislated certain hours when alcohol can and cannot be sold to consumers. Some states have state wide restrictions, and others also allow for counties and municipalities to determine their own alcohol sales times. Most either do not allow, or only allow limited, sales of alcohol on Sundays.

In Alabama, for example, it is illegal to sell alcohol after 2 A.M. on Sunday. *See* Code of Alabama §28-3A-25. In New York, it is illegal to sell alcohol between 3 A.M. and 8 A.M. on Sunday. *See* New York Alcohol Beverage Control Law §105-A. In California, sales are permitted only between 6 A.M. and 2 A.M. every day. *See* California Business and Professions Code §25631. Vermont has different rules for brewpubs and restaurants (8 A.M. to 2 A.M.) than for stores selling beer and wine (6 A.M. to 12 A.M.). *See* Vermont Statutes Tile 7, Chapter 3, §62. Most of the states, even if there is a state-wide restriction, allow counties and municipalities to place additional restrictions on the time and days of alcohol sales.

No More Questions

Conclusion. Or, the summary.

The alcohol industry is one of the most heavily regulated industries in the United States. Brewers must navigate through a maze of federal, state, and local laws, rules, and regulations before they are even licensed to make and sell beer. Once a brewery is producing beer, there are additional mazes to conquer to sell the beer. There are label and advertising restrictions to contend with. Distribution systems are mandated by the states, and there are several layers of laws and regulations related to trade practices. Once the beer is sold, there are even more mazes to navigate to pay taxes.

Brewers should not endeavor to start breweries lightly. It is a complicated, and often expensive, process. It is, however, very rewarding for many brewers. All brewers should be aware of the laws and issues facing them when opening or expanding a brewery. The issues will often inform how the brewer sets up the business model for the brewery. Understanding the laws will also help the brewer create a more specific business plan and budget, rather than changing the plan as new issues arise. While this publication has not covered all aspects of the laws that apply to breweries, we hope that you now understand the laws surrounding breweries enough to begin planning a successful business model.

Simply understanding the laws is not enough. Brewers should consult and work with the TTB and their state alcohol control divisions at each step of the way. The TTB officers are often a wealth of information on all aspects of the laws and regulations pertaining to breweries. It is also important for brewers to obtain the counsel and advice of competent licensed legal and financial professionals in their home state before and during any brewery operations.

Table 1

SOME POTENTIAL COSTS

Below is a table listing some (but definitely not all) costs that may be associated with opening and operating a brewery. Manufacturing and similar operational costs are not included in the table below, as these types of costs will vary widely from brewery to brewery. Costs of professional services (legal, financial, marketing) are also not included in the table below.

This table is not (nor is it intended to be) inclusive; it is only provided to show examples of the kinds of fees a commercial brewer should look out for. There will be many additional costs and fees associated with setting up the business itself and with running and insuring the business.

Cost
Federal Bond along with Brewer's Notice
State License Fee (and any additional administrative fees)
State Bond
County License Fee (and any administrative fees)
Municipal License Fee (and any administrative fees)

Other State fees (industry representatives, label and advertisement fees, etc.)
Responsible Vendor Program fees
Federal Excise Taxes
State Excise Taxes
State, County, and Municipal sales taxes
Insurance costs (general liability, casualty, dram shop (liquor) liability)
Real estate costs (lease or ownership, insurance, improvements)
Costs of tastings (some states require that the entity on who's property the tasting is being held pay for all costs, including the beer)

Table 2

FEDERAL TIED HOUSE EXCEPTIONS

The table below lists only the federal exceptions to the federal tied house laws and regulations. The states have similar tied house laws and regulations and similar exceptions. The laws and regulations, however, differ from state to state and even if the federal laws or another state's laws allow for one exception, it does not mean that your particular state will allow for the same exception. It is important to understand the laws of your state and consult with a competent licensed attorney in your state regarding any prohibited trade practices.

Things of value that may be given to retailers:	Regulations 27 CFR
Product Displays - provided displays do not exceed $300 per brand at any one establishment	§6.83
Point Of Sale & Consumer Advertising - posters, inside signs, clocks, calendars, menus, product list, etc.; retailer must not be paid or credited by industry member in order to use these materials	§6.84
Temporary Retailers - not engaged in business for more than 4 consecutive days per event and not more than 5 events per year	§6.85

Things of value that may be given to retailers:	Regulations 27 CFR
Equipment & Supplies - glassware, dispensing accessories, ice, etc.; sold to retailer for not less than cost, and price is collected within 30 days	§6.88
Samples - 3 gallons of malt beverages; provided not purchased within previous 12 months	§6.91
Newspaper Cuts	§6.92
Combination Packaging - combining distribution and packaging of alcohol and non-alcoholic beverages	§6.93
Educational Seminars - sponsored by industry member	§6.94
Consumer Tasting - at retailer establishment	§6.95
Consumer Promotions - coupons and direct offerings to consumers	§6.96
Advertising Service - where two or more unaffiliated retailers selling industry member products are listed in an advertisement	§6.98
Stocking Rotation & Pricing - provided other industry members' products are not altered or disturbed	§6.99
Participation in Retailer Association Activities	§6.100
Merchandise - groceries, pharmaceuticals, etc., sold at fair market value; not combined with sale of alcoholic beverages	§6.101
Outside Signs - provided it bears conspicuous advertising matter about product/industry member and costs does not exceed $400, and the retailer is not compensated	§6.102

Table 3

BREWER'S REPORT OF OPERATIONS and DAILY RECORDS ITEMS

Note that all items required to be tracked need to be tracked in barrels or fractions thereof. *See* §§ 27 CFR 25.156 and 157 for a breakdown of barrel equivalents for kegs and bottles.

Items Required
Each material received and used
Beer produced (including water added after production is determined)
Beer transferred for and returned from bottling
Beer transferred for and returned from racking
Beer bottled
Beer racked
Beer removed from the brewery for consumption or sale
Beer removed from the brewery without payment of tax
Beer used for laboratory samples at the brewery
Beer consumed at the brewery (tasting rooms)
Beer returned to the brewery after it was removed
Beer reconditioned or used as material

Items Required
Beer destroyed
Beer received from other breweries or received from pilot brewing plants
Beer lost due to breakage, theft, casualty, or other unusual cause
Beer shortages, along with an explanation
Beer removed for exportation
Beer on hand at the beginning and ending of any reporting period

LaVergne, TN USA
10 February 2011
215929LV00001BA/13/P